1001
DOT-TO-DOT

DAY OF THE
DEAD

INCREDIBLE PUZZLES
TO LIVEN UP YOUR DAY

THUNDER BAY
P·R·E·S·S

San Diego, California

Welcome to *1001 Dot-to-Dot: Day of the Dead* and the challenge waiting for you! To reveal each image, you'll join together 1001 numbered dots in order, and when you're finished connecting the dots, you can use coloring tools—pens, pencils, crayons, highlighters—to bring the image to life.

As you complete each puzzle, you'll learn about a festival that has its origins in a world of human sacrifice. That culture is now long gone, but the goddess of the dead was not forgotten, and she evolved through the years. By the beginning of the twentieth century, she had become an icon of protest, and a revolution followed.

Today the Day of the Dead is a celebration that unites a country, and it is traveling across the world. Perhaps that's because it makes remembering the dead a joyful experience, a time for sharing memories and laughing, rather than a grim experience as it is viewed in many other cultures.

Where the dots are clustered, we've sometimes used darker colors for the dots and their corresponding number to help you out. If you need further assistance, all the solutions are printed at the back of the book.

The Day of the Dead is a festival that's been hundreds of years in the making, and the word that describes it best is "exuberance." An altar strewn with Aztec marigolds is a dazzle of oranges and golds. Catrina, the Lady of the Dead, parades in finery that's taken months to prepare.

The artists who create *calaveras* (sugar skulls) compete for awards. It's color, color, color by day and night. And that's what your puzzles will need after the dots are connected: color. Joining the dots to reveal the image is just the start!

1

The Day of the Dead is a tradition that has its roots in the culture of the Aztecs, warrior people who dominated Mexico and Central America until the arrival of the Spanish *conquistadores* in the sixteenth century.

2

Their dead journeyed, so the Aztecs believed, to Mictlan, an underworld located to the north. Its queen was Mictecacihuatl, who was born in the days before the first humans, when the world was still young.

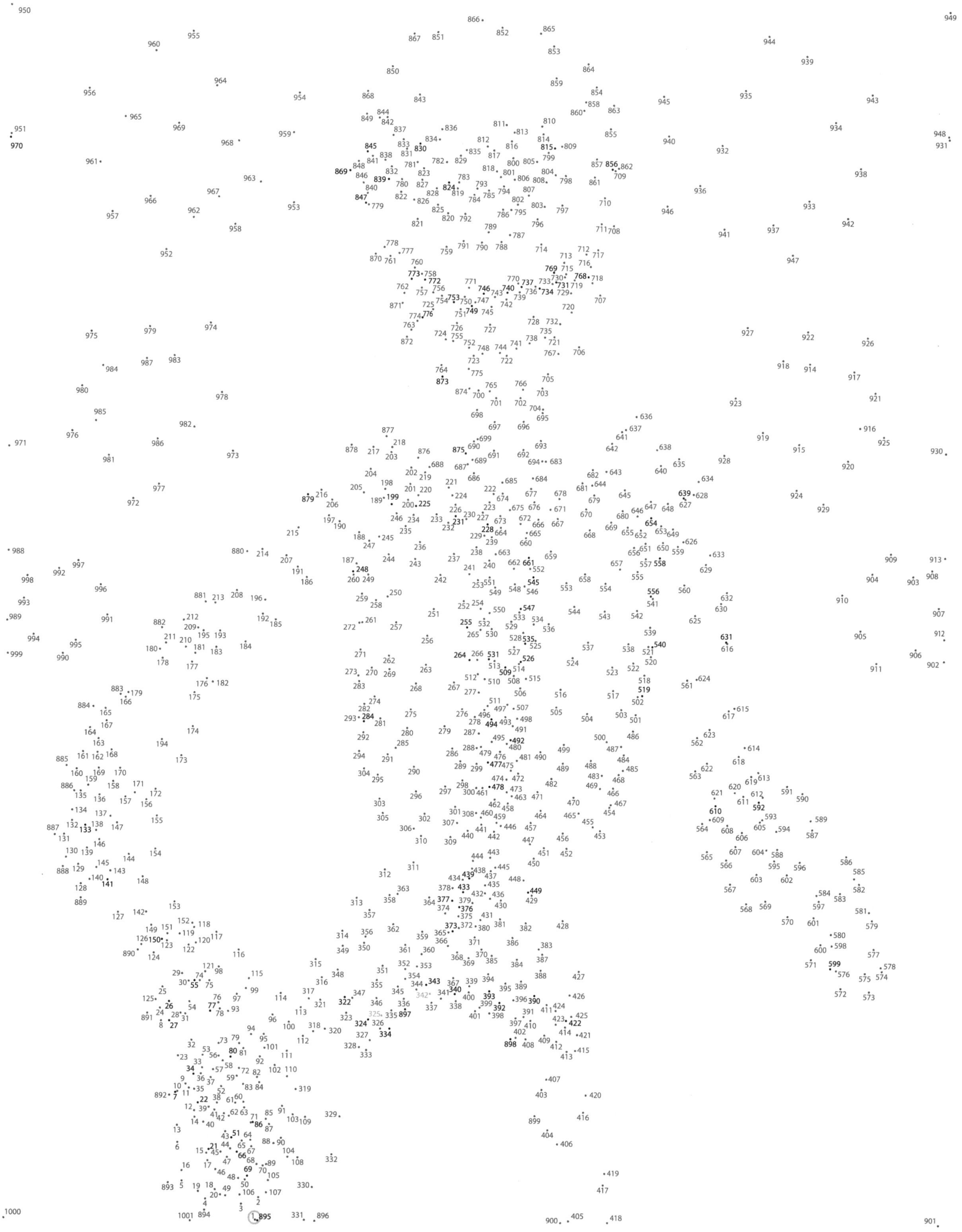

3

While still an infant, Mictecacihuatl was sacrificed to the underworld. Deprived of life, she continued to grow, and is now an elegant skeleton with considerable powers. Her role is to watch over the bones of the dead.

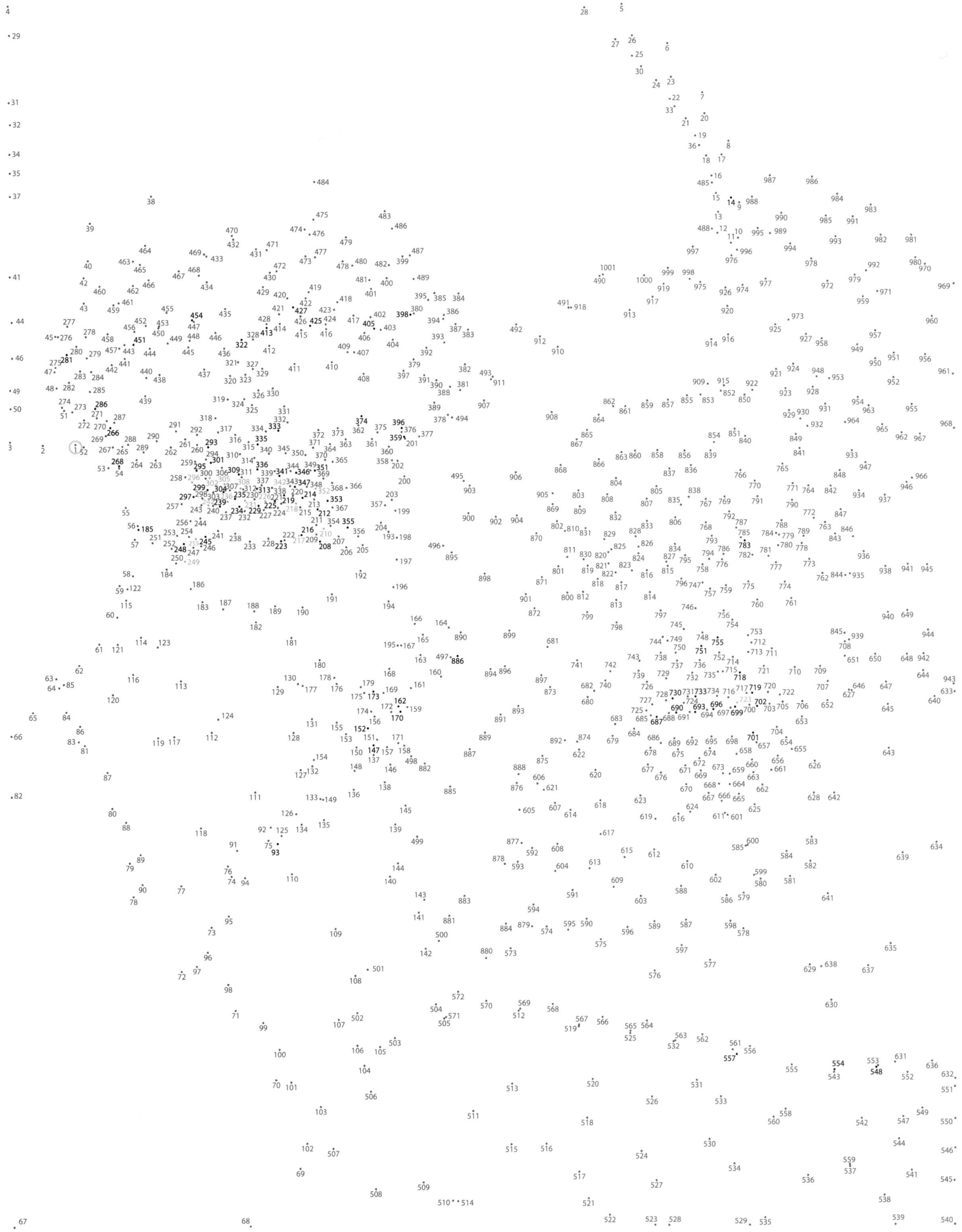

4

Mictecacihuatl once failed in this role, and Xolotl, the god of sickness and lightning, stole a corpse. From this, modern human beings were created. If a human corpse is ever stolen, the gods will create a new and terrible race.

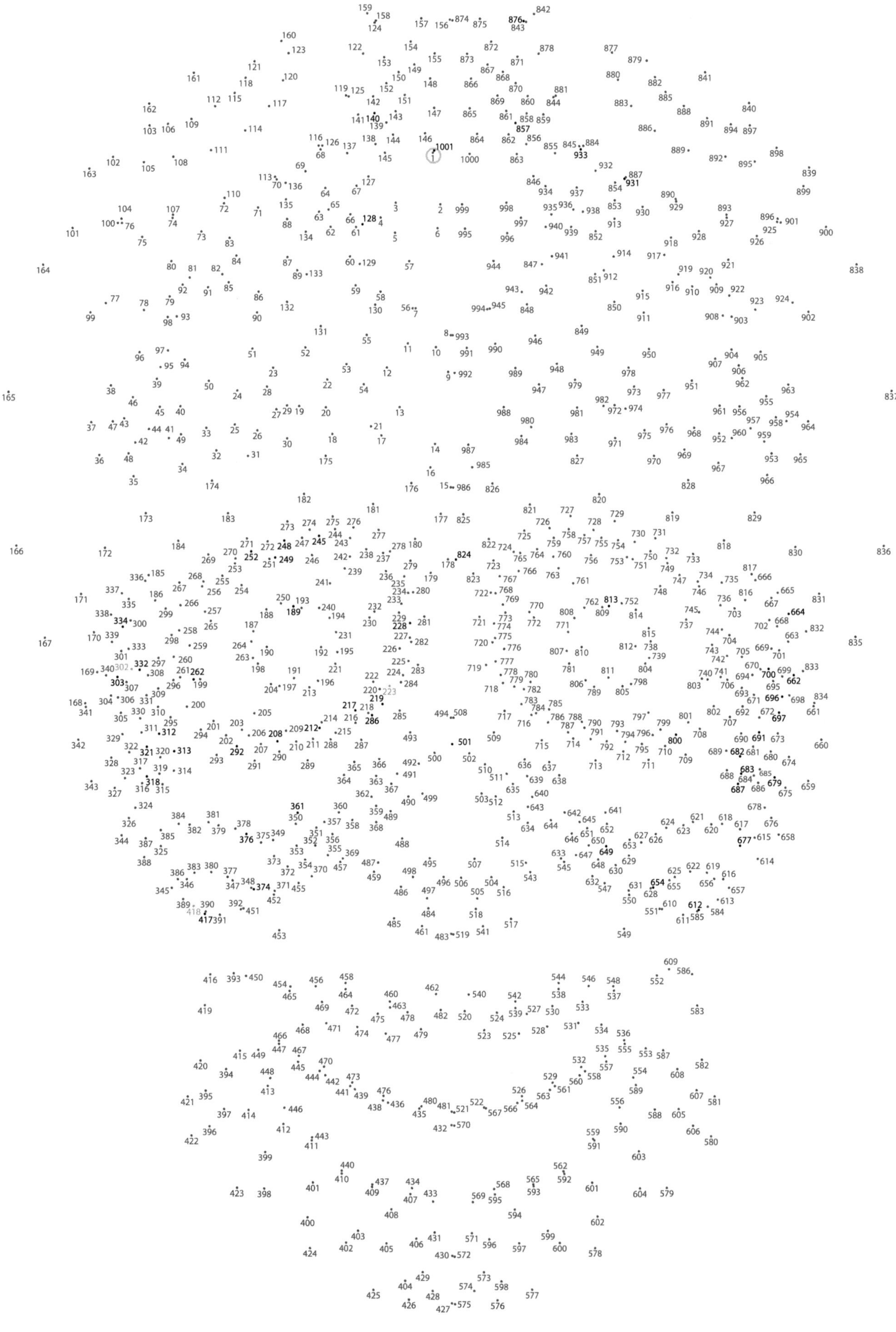

5

Mictecacihuatl loves flowers, and the Aztec marigold—or *flor de muertos*—is sacred to her. The scent of their blooms can wake the souls of the dead and bring them back each year to the land of the living.

6

Then, as now, altars were festooned with the marigolds—a flower that grows wild across Central America. Petals are sometimes strewn from the front door to the altar, leading the souls to the heart of the family home.

7

The altar has three levels, said to represent Heaven, Earth, and Purgatory—
which reveals the influence of the Catholic Church. In the underworld of the
Aztecs, there were nine levels, and the journey through them all was hard.

8

The Aztecs dominated the region for centuries. The Spanish conquered them in less than three years. They brought with them their Catholic traditions, including All Saints' Eve, All Saints' Day, and All Souls' Day. The latter commemorates all who have died, especially family members.

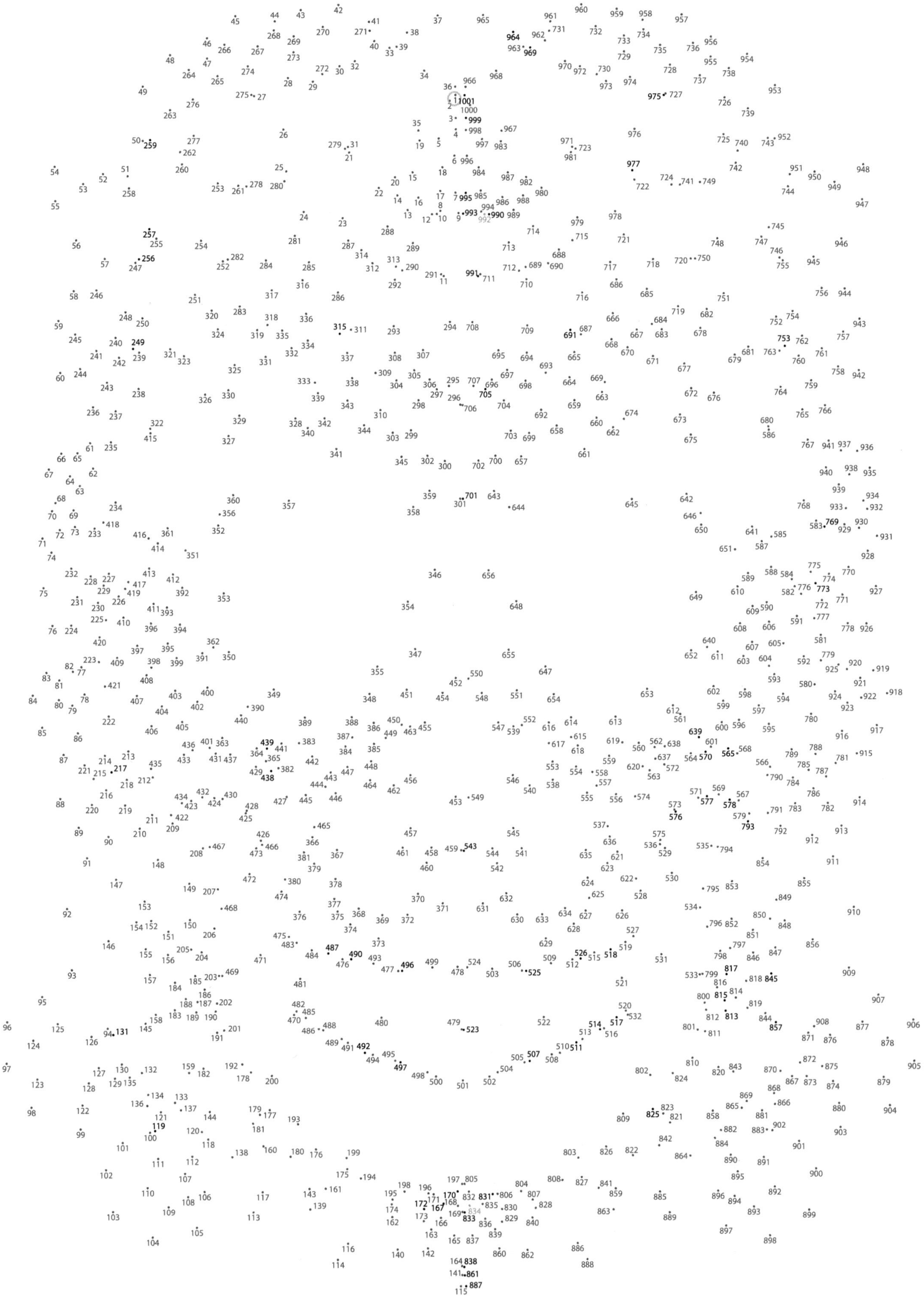

9

Sharing a similar purpose, the Aztec and Christian festivals gradually became intertwined, and today the Day of the Dead is celebrated on November 2. The Aztec traditions continue, though, with each family coming together to build an altar at home.

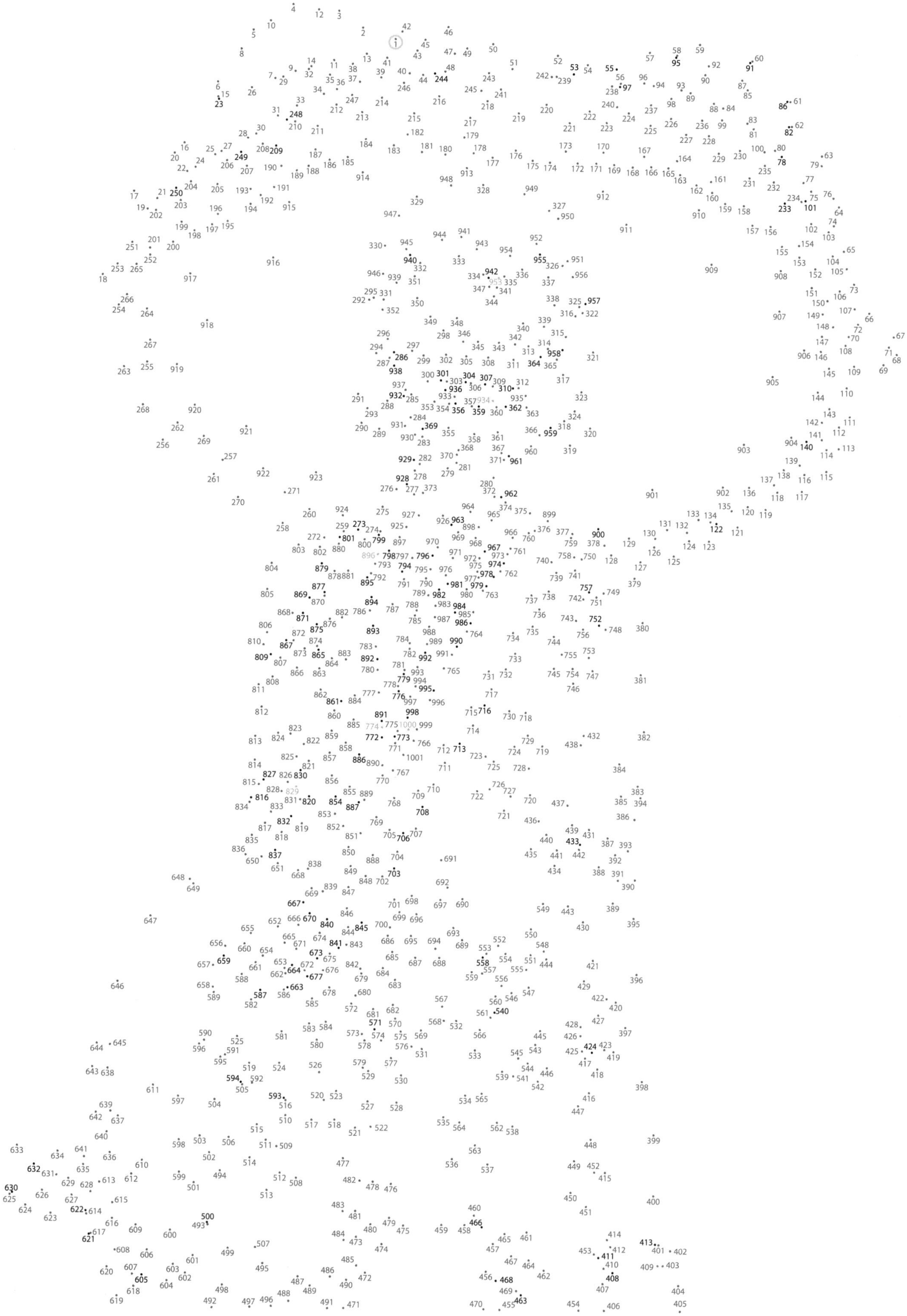

10

Across Mexico, the rituals and their meaning change from region to region. In Michoacán, for example, the festival coincides with the migration of the monarch butterflies returning from the north. They are believed to be the returning souls.

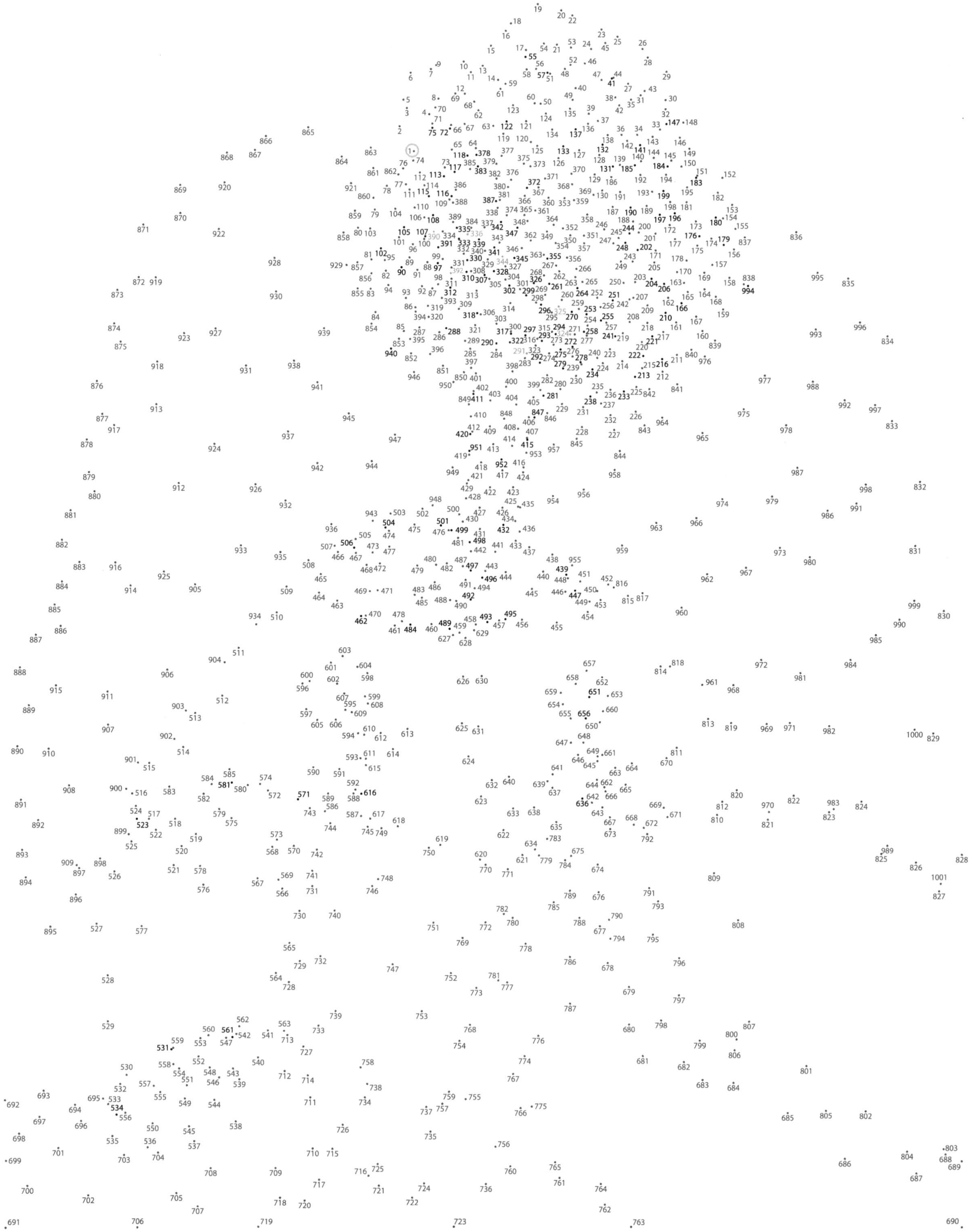

11

What is constant throughout Mexico is the importance of the day—families may spend more than two months' income to celebrate their dead relatives. The expense is justified: souls who are happy protect the living and bring good luck.

12

Souls who have been overlooked may seek vengeance, particularly if they compare notes with other spirits whose families have been generous. It is said that those who ignore their dead relatives will soon fall ill—and they may even die.

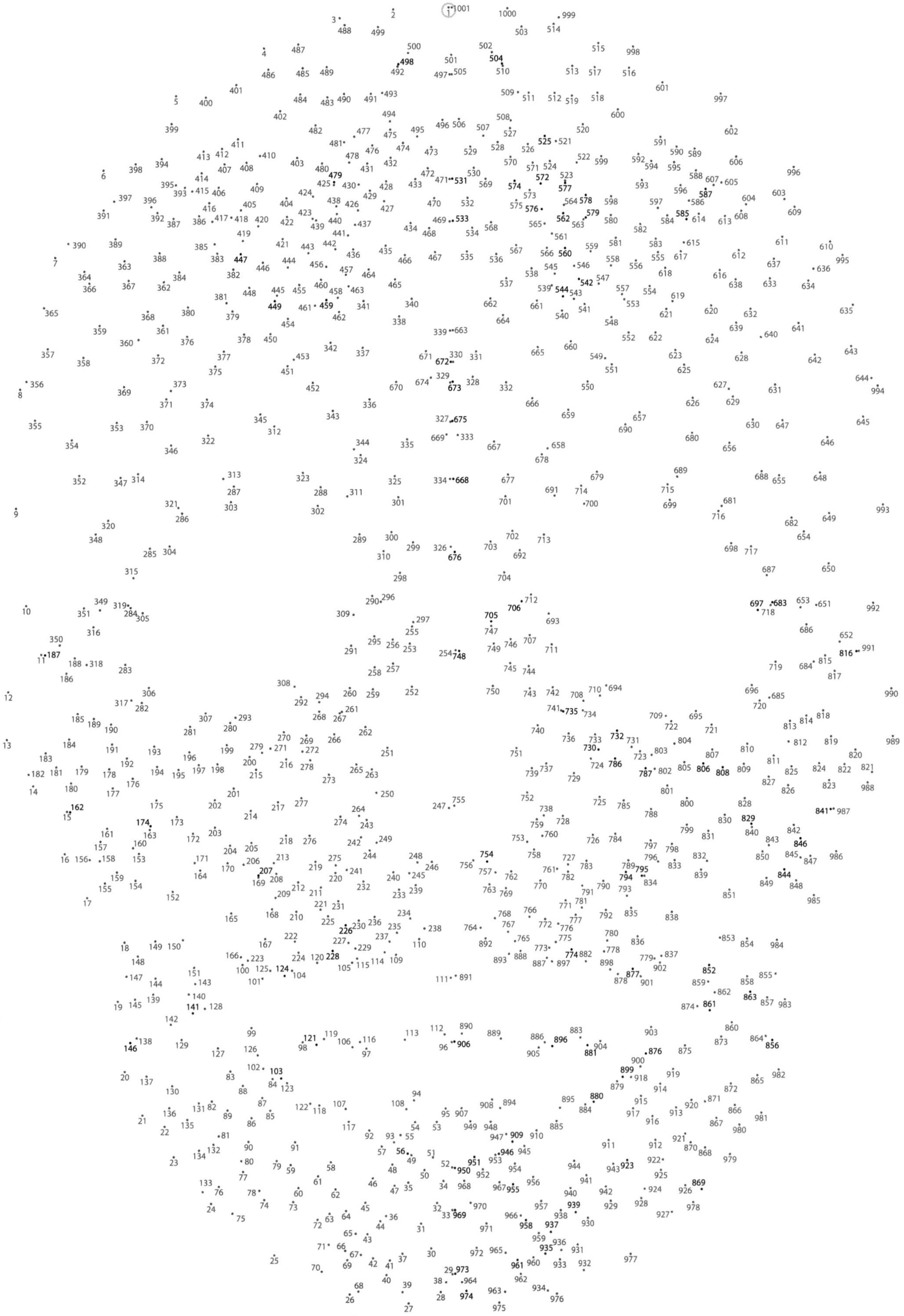

13

The whole family comes together to prepare the altar, and inevitably talk about who has died. Stories are remembered, jokes are told, and for children this is an opportunity to talk about dying without getting upset.

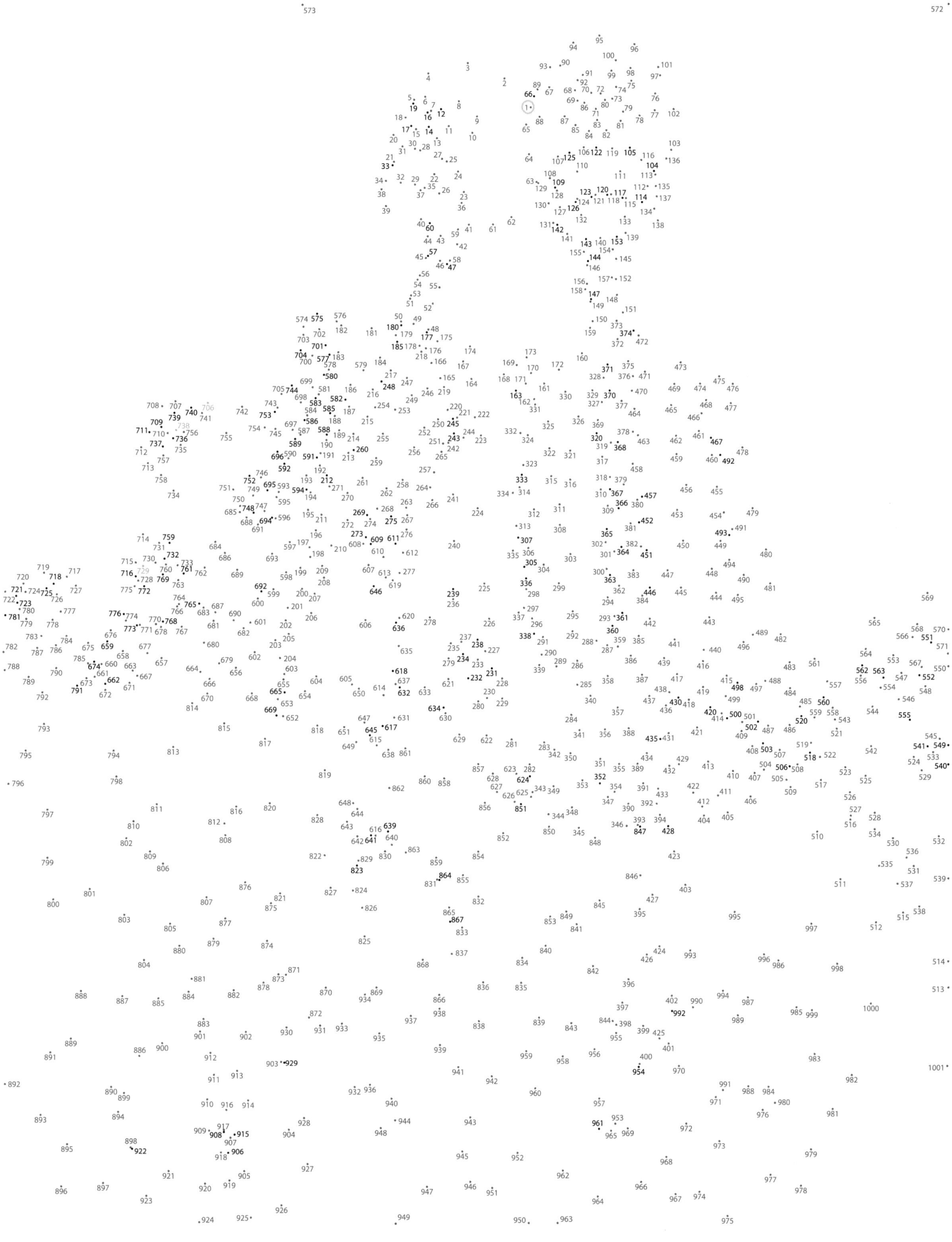

14

Along with photographs, treats are laid out for the dead—a shot of tequila or, for a child, a favorite toy. The dead may want to refresh themselves after their long journey, so a mirror and a washbasin are essential.

15

The dead may also be hungry and thirsty, so lots of water and food will be on offer. *Pan de muerto*, or "dead man's bread," is a soft bread (like brioche) that is sometimes iced white, the color of bones.

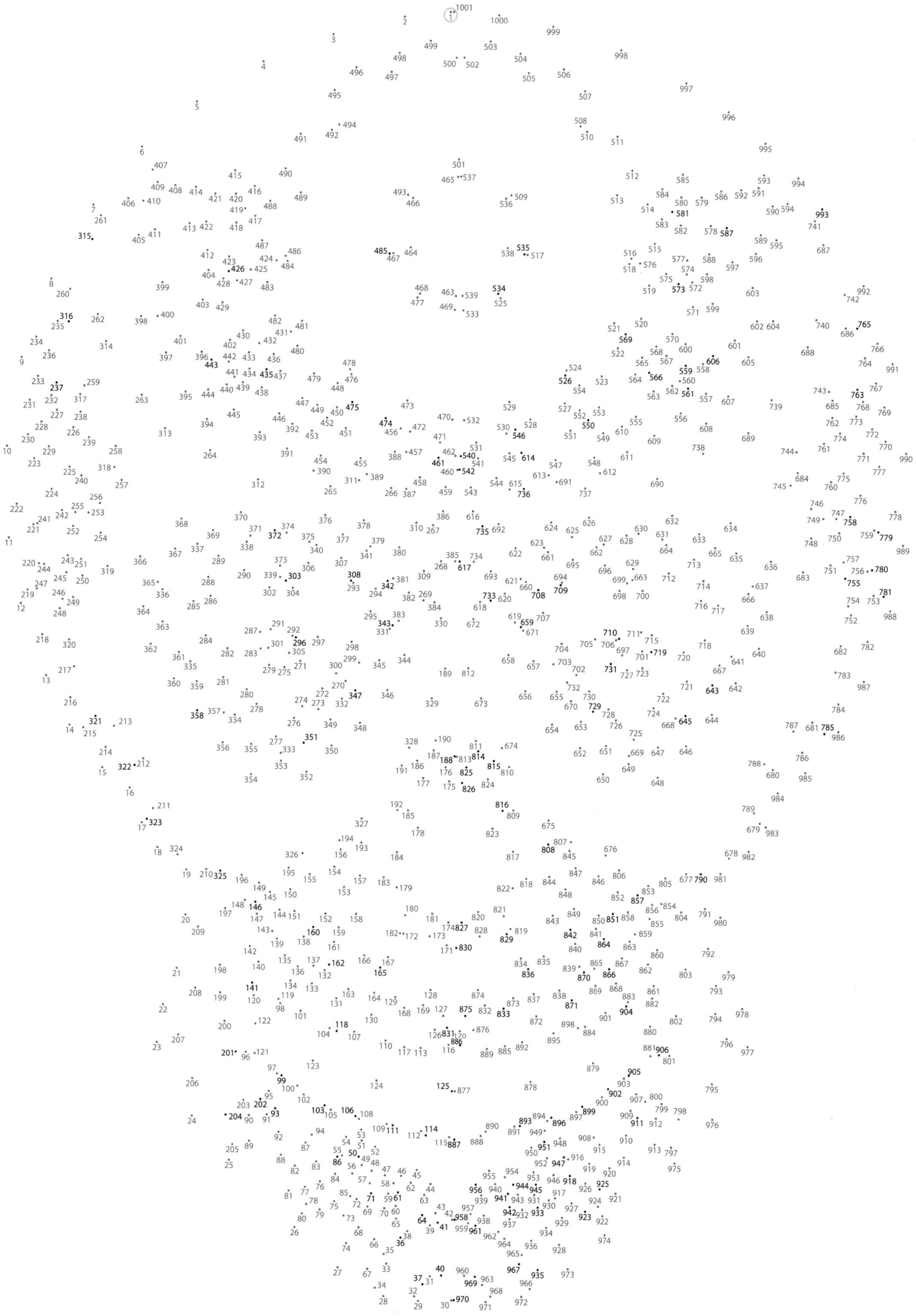

16

There is a theory that *pan de muerto* reveals the influence of the Spanish. They introduced wheat to the Americas, and were appalled by the human sacrifices. A sweet bread, sometimes shaped into a human figure, seemed like a good compromise.

This is a connect-the-dots puzzle page consisting of numbered dots (1–1001) scattered across the page. The content is not readable prose.

17

Pan de muerto is not just for the dead. It's a treat for the living too—to the extent that in some regions bakers sell it for months before the day. Of course, there's nothing to stop you from making your own at any time.

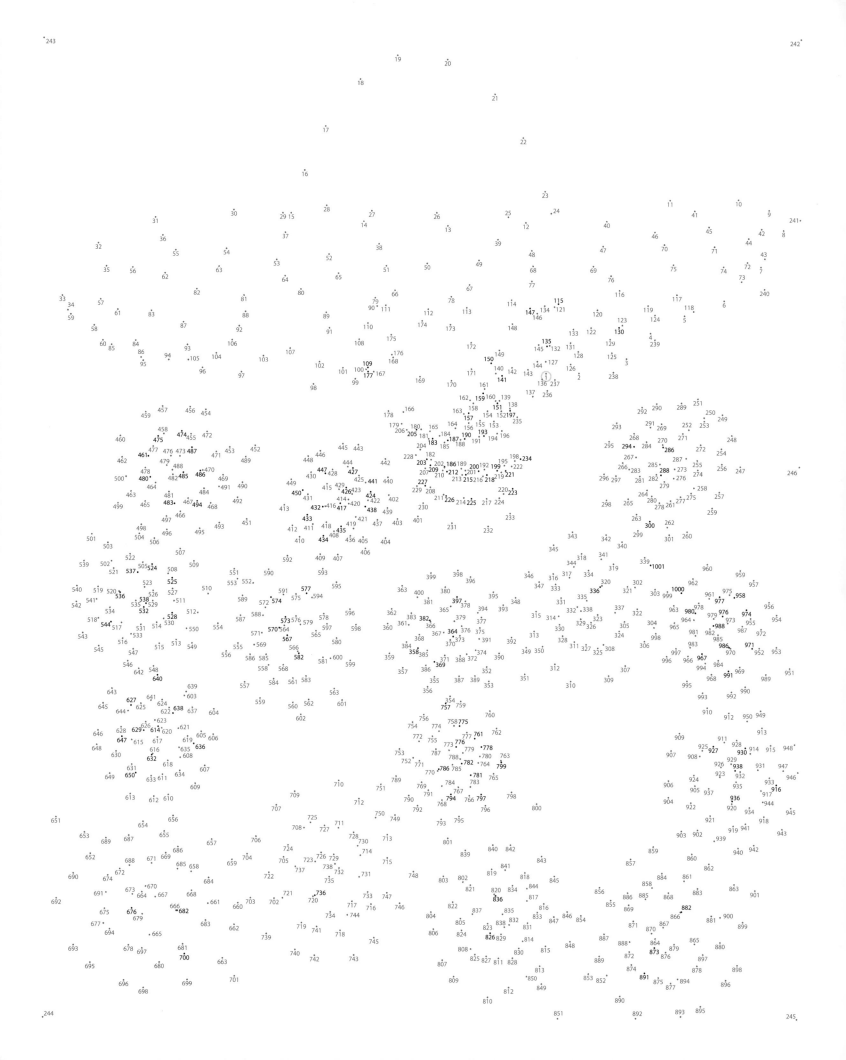

18

Marigolds are placed all over the altar. Fresh, dried, paper, or silk—the more, the better. The same goes for the *calaveras*. These are human skulls, usually made of sugar, though not necessarily meant to be eaten.

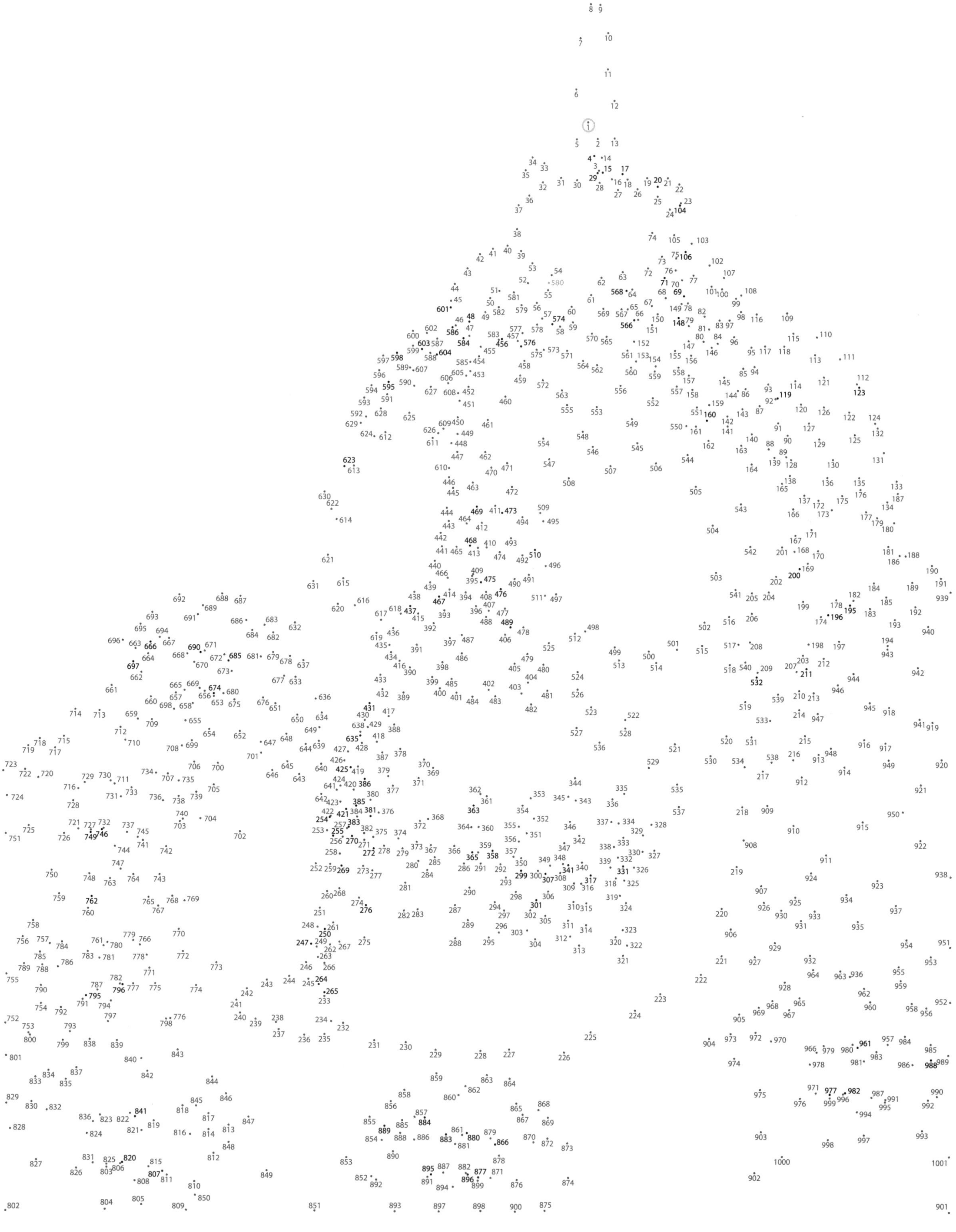

19

Calaveras have been made since the seventeenth century, and the traditional methods are time-consuming. Their creators may take up to six months preparing for the season, and the designs may include beads, feathers, and even sequins.

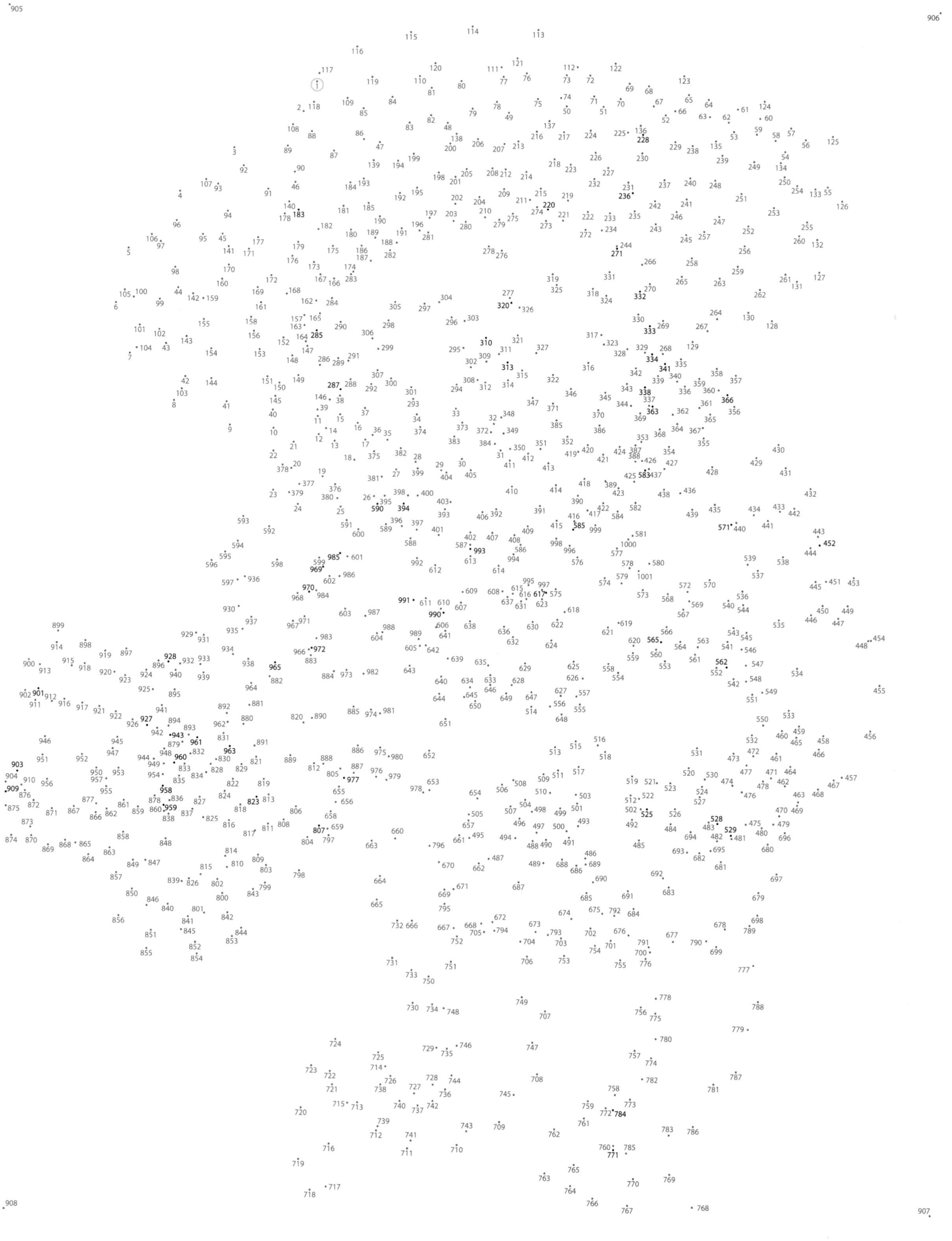

20

If you want to decorate your own sugar skulls, you'll need frosting—lots of it, and in as many colors as possible. And you'll also need plenty of time. Not just for the decorations but also for the frosting to dry.

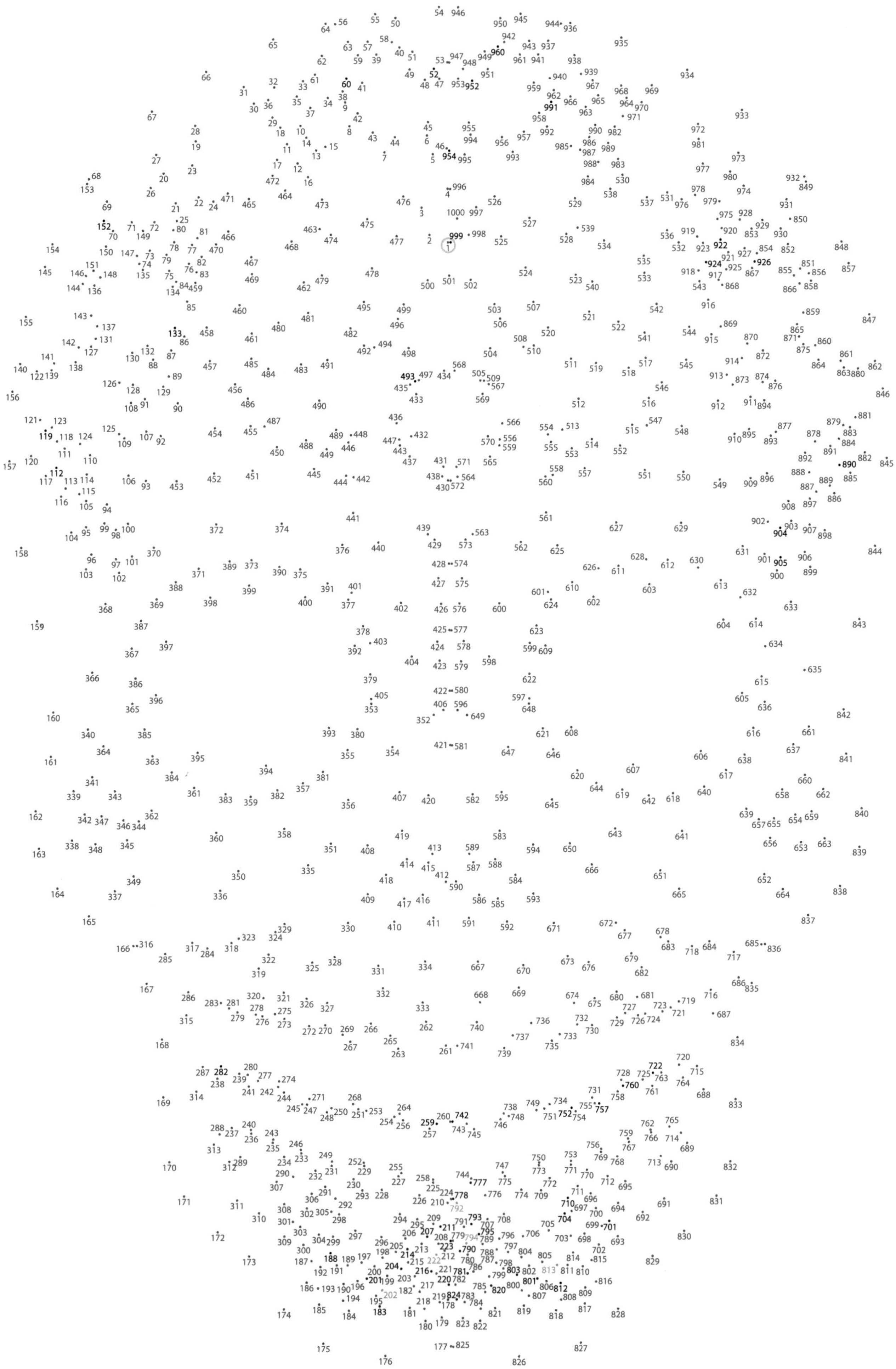

21

There are, of course, skulls for eating. Some are made from sugar, often flavored with vanilla; others are made from chocolate. And if a skull makes you squeamish, try a coffin instead. Or a skeleton. Or a cross.

22

It was the Spanish who introduced sugar, after realizing that they had conquered an area perfect for its production. They also introduced the European tradition of making religious decorations from sugar—which was now plentiful and cheap.

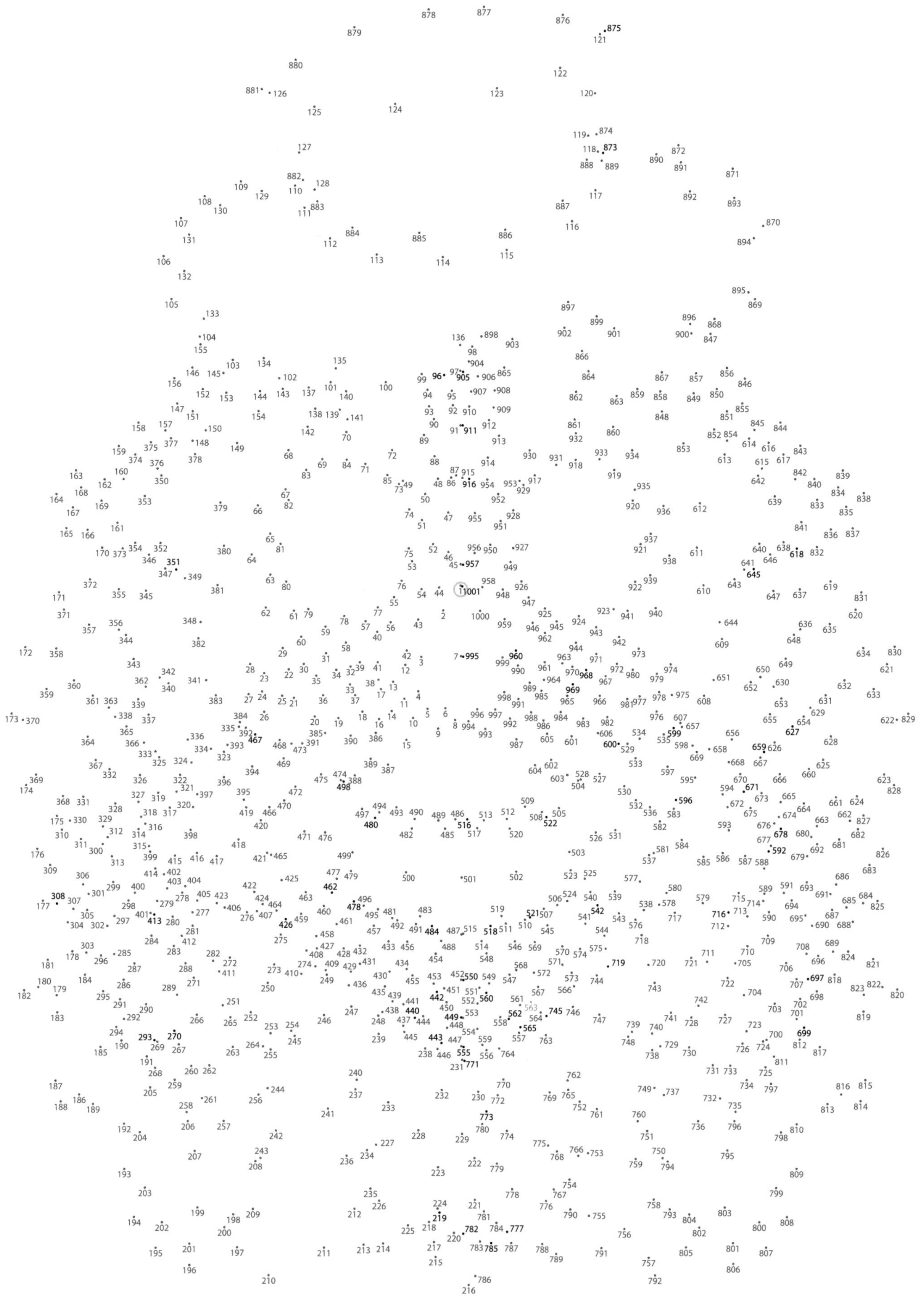

23

At the Feria del Alfeñique, which takes place every year in Toluca, the makers of sugar skulls compete for awards. From mid-October to the beginning of November, they sell their wares under the arches of Los Portales.

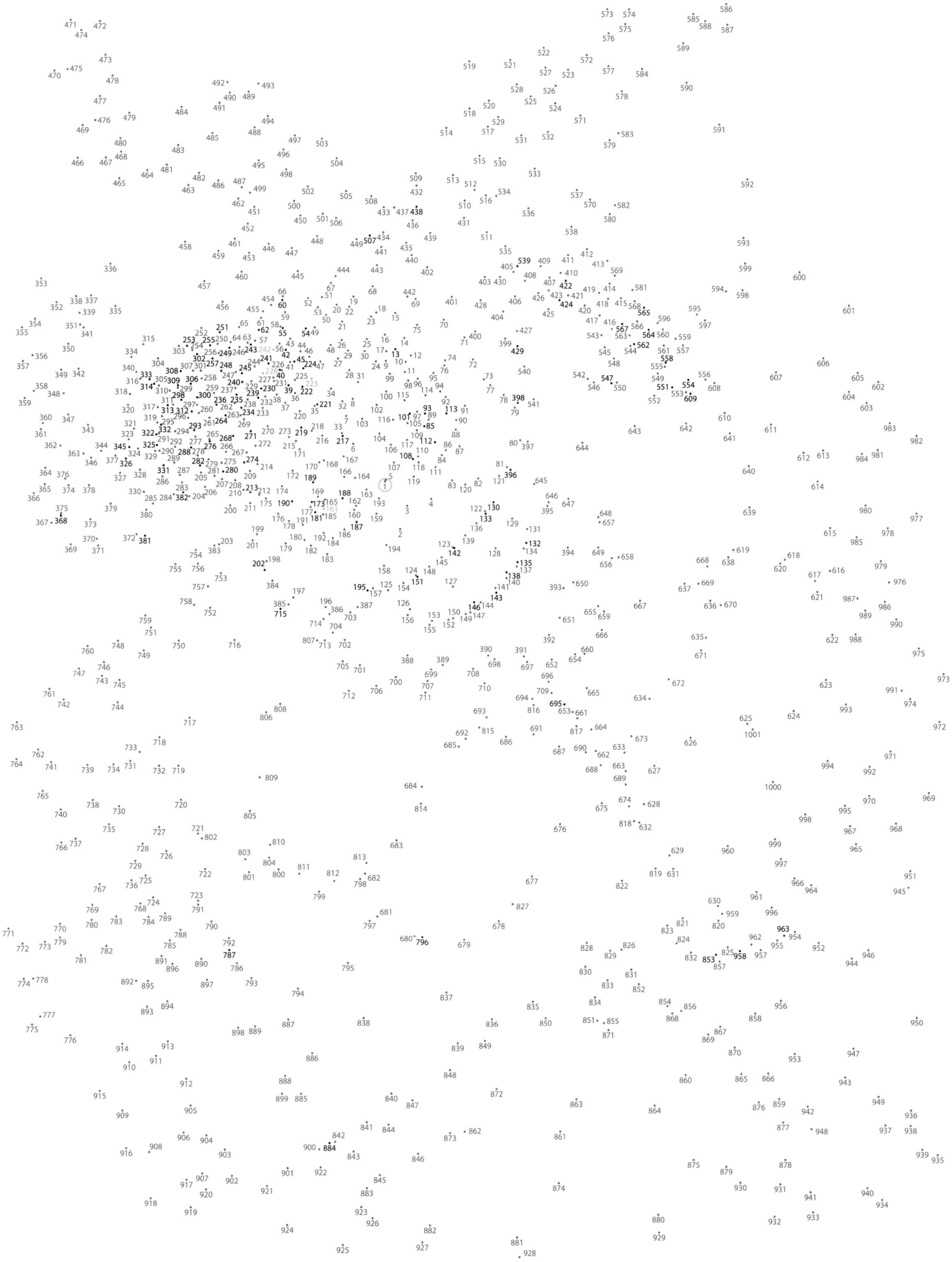

24

A skull placed on an altar traditionally carries the names of the dead on its forehead. A small skull is for a dead child, a full-size skull for adults. Once the altar has been taken down, these skulls are often thrown away.

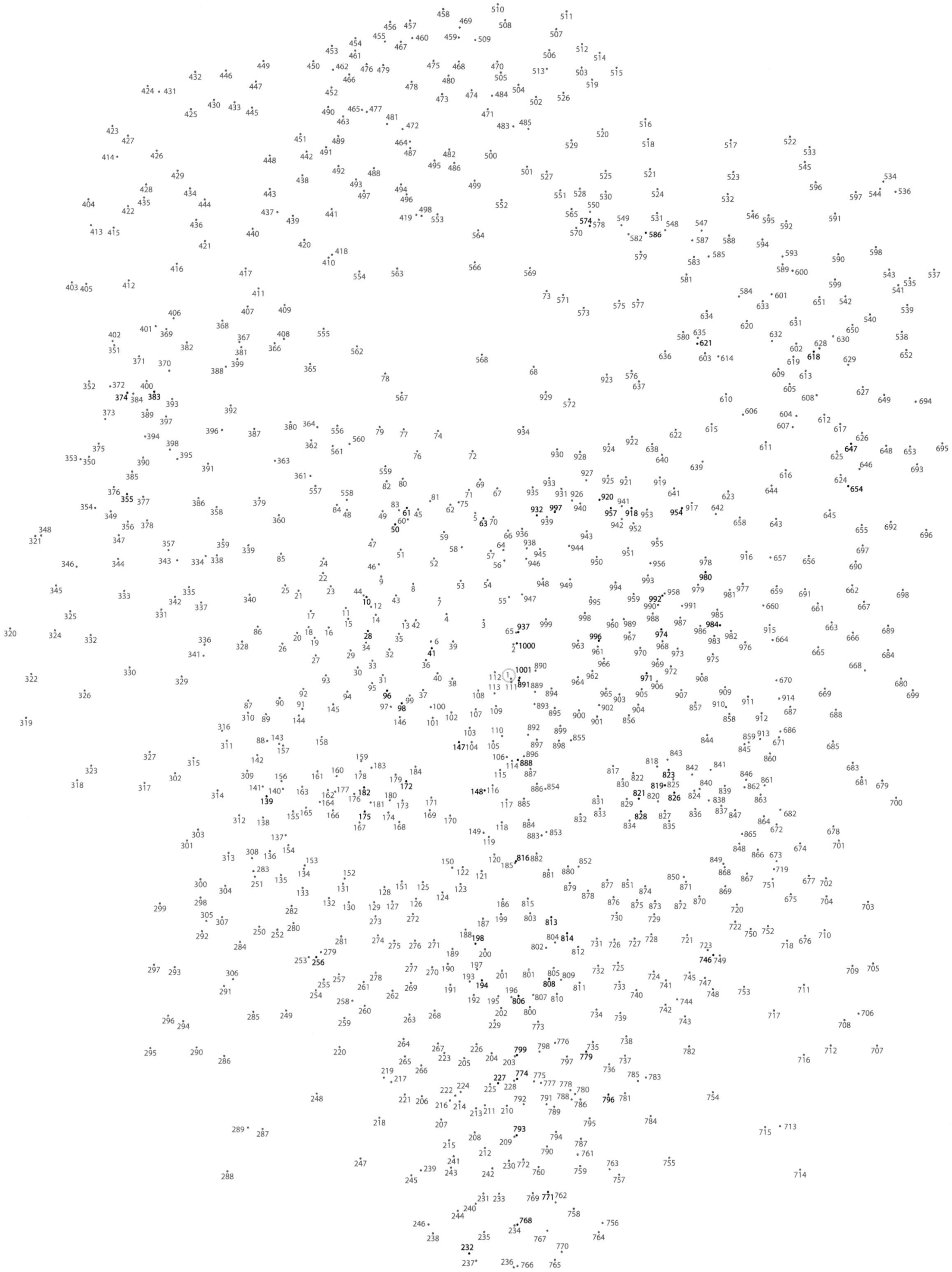

25

It is traditional to burn copal on the altar. Copal is a tree resin, burned at
ceremonies for thousands of years by both Aztecs and Mayans. Its purpose
is to bring together heaven and earth.

26

Día de los Muertos actually refers only to the final day, November 2. The previous day is dedicated to children and is known as *El Día de los Angelitos* (little angels). It recalls the Aztec Little Feast for the Dead.

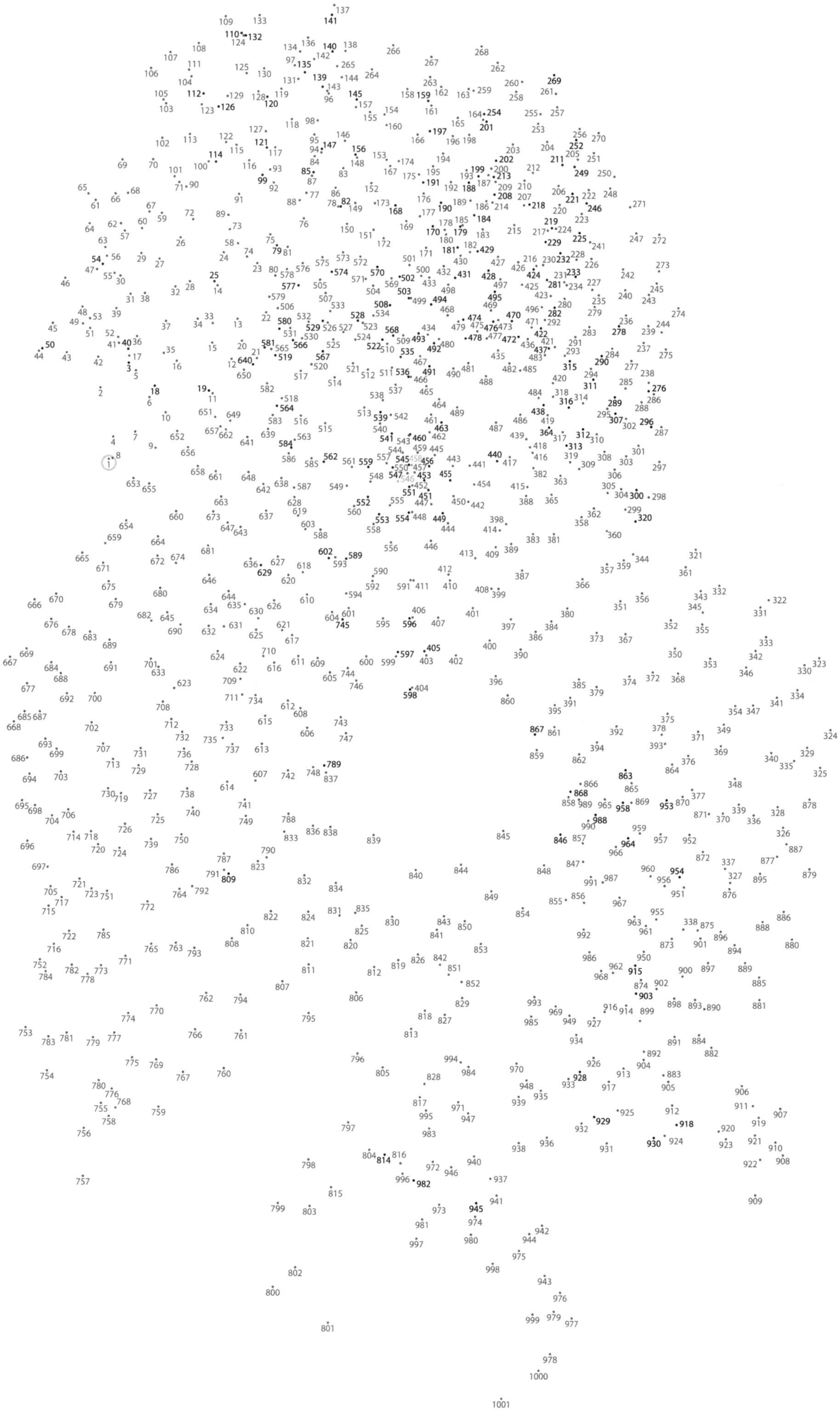

27

The *angelitos* are said to return to their families at midnight on October 31.
In some regions, the family will wait at the cemetery all night to welcome the
children the moment they return to earth.

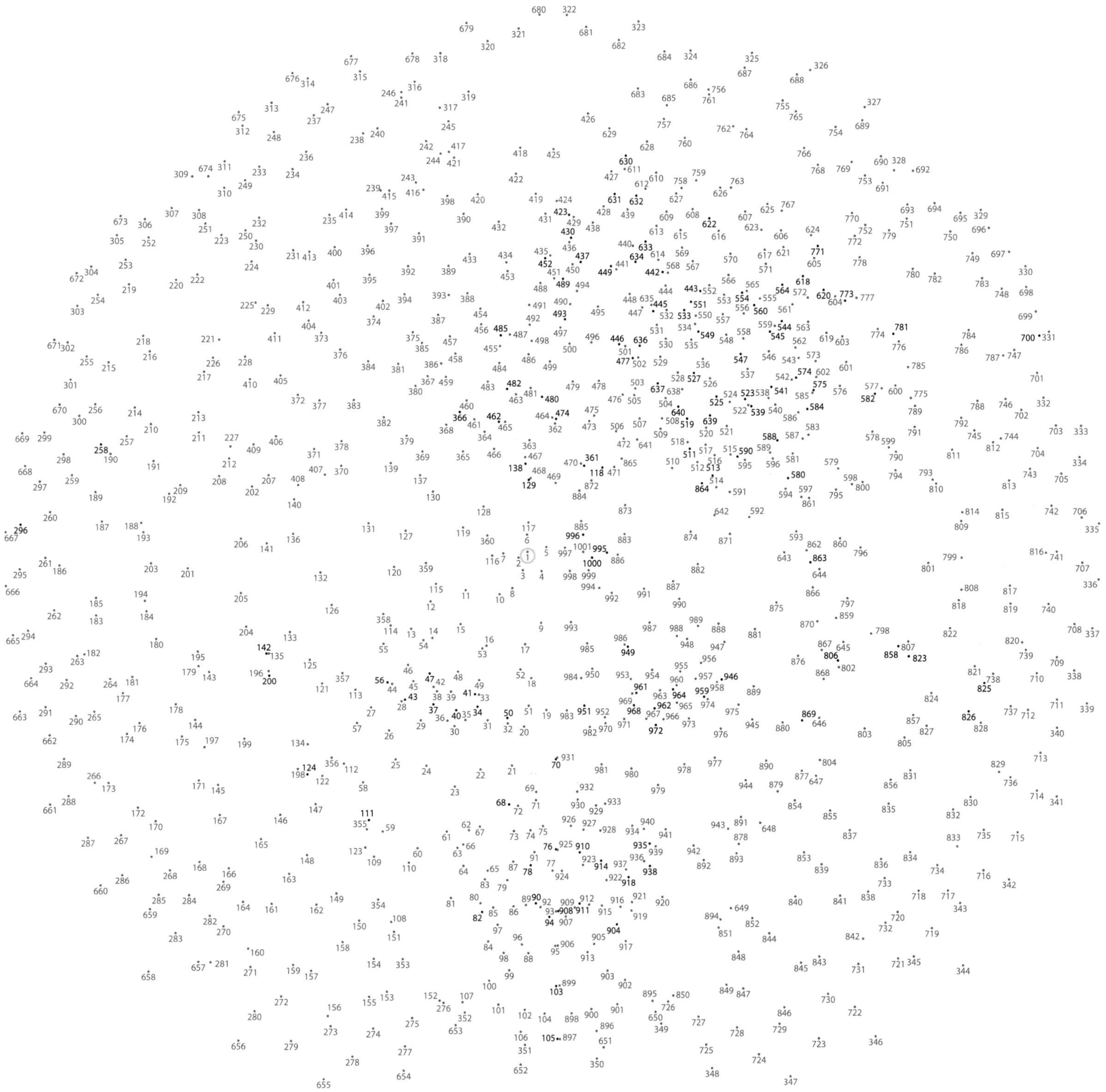

28

This is not a time of mourning. Rather, it is a time to celebrate the links between the living and the dead. Indeed, families believe that their *angelitos* will now intercede for them with God.

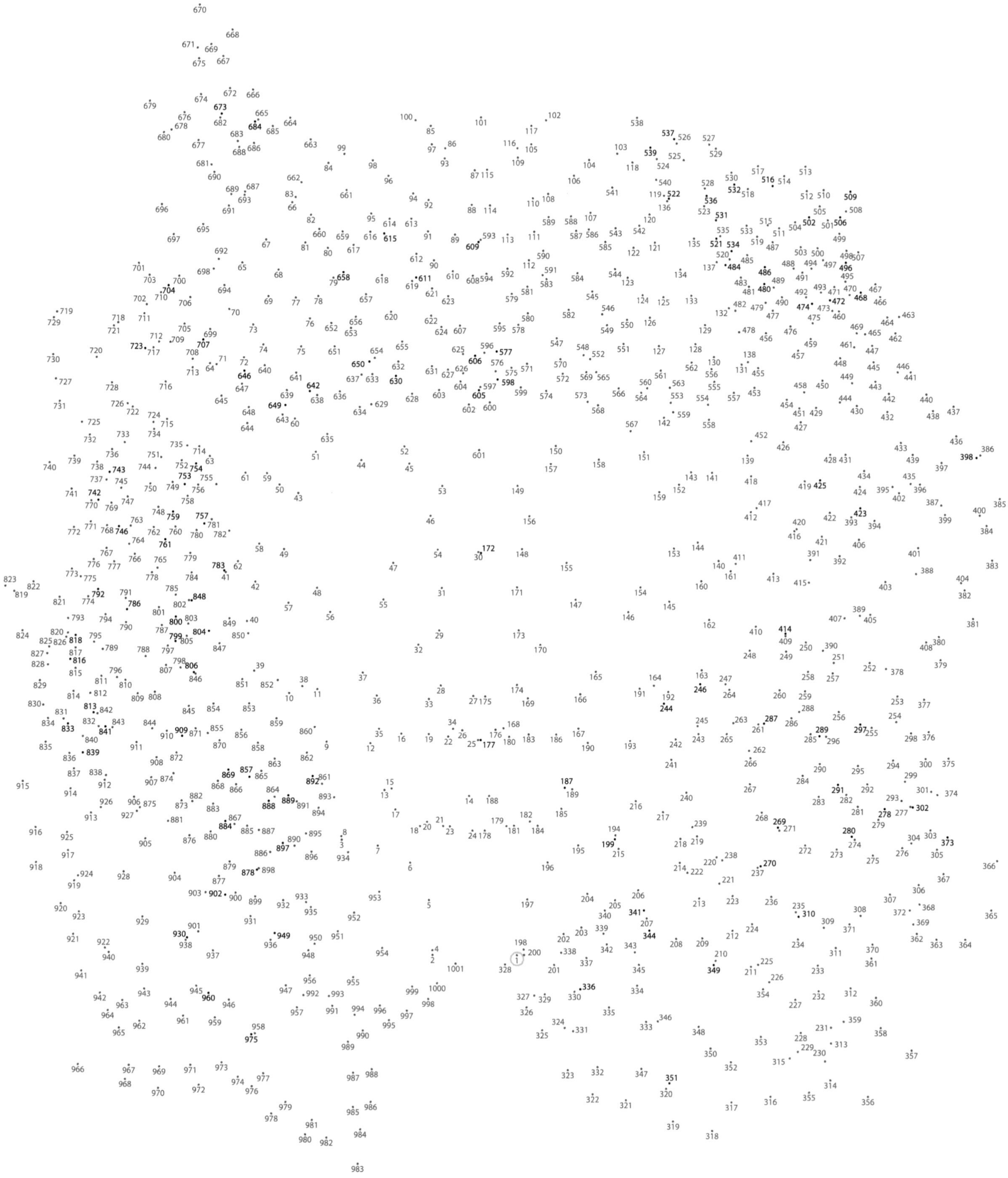

29

Adult souls return on November 2, and this is the day when families visit the cemetery. Here the village band may be playing while tombs are cleaned and decorated, and families may then share a picnic.

30

The day has come to be associated with Catrina. An elegantly dressed skeleton, she was originally meant to satirize those Mexicans, particularly aristocrats, who denied their heritages and preferred to pass as Europeans.

31

Catrina was the creation of José Guadalupe Posada, a Mexican illustrator protesting against the conditions that would lead to the Mexican Revolution. As the rich took control of the land, *campesinos* (peasant farmers) struggled to make a living.

32

Posada's image is a skull wearing an extravagantly decorated hat. Later, the artist Diego Rivera painted her full length in a mural where she stands center stage. Strolling through a park, she is surrounded by notable figures from Mexican history.

33

The mural, titled *Dream of a Sunday Afternoon in the Alameda Central,* has a darker side, though. Catrina seems not to notice the police officer confronting an indigenous family, or the horse trampling a man as he is shot in the face.

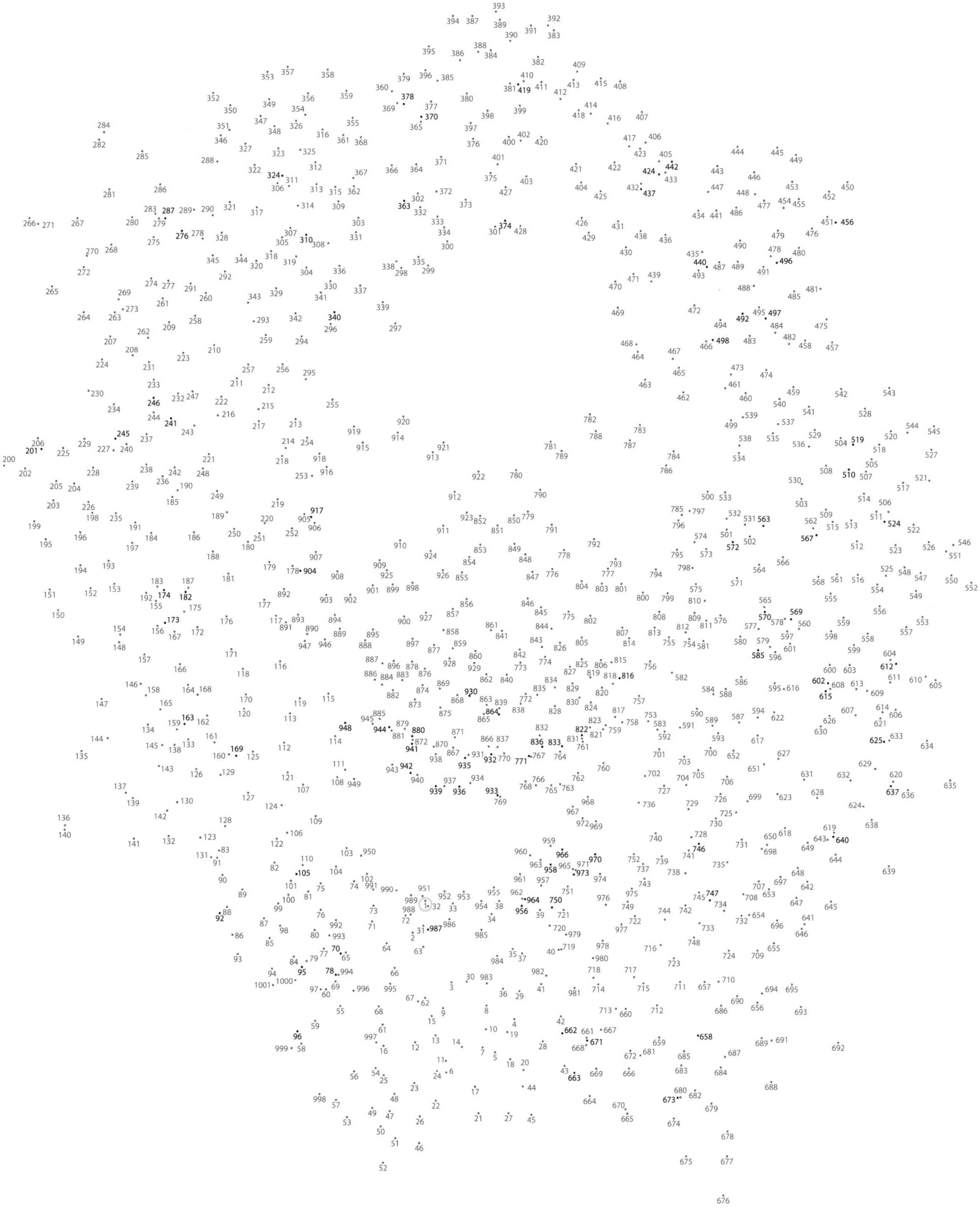

34

It may also be Rivera who gave Catrina her name. In Spanish, *catrin* means both "well dressed" and "honored." The original satirical intent is clear. Today she is the mistress of ceremonies, the woman everyone wants to be.

35

In her finery, Catrina serves as a reminder that death comes to us all—and breaks down the barriers between rich and poor. At the same time, a beautifully dressed skeleton looks ridiculous. We respect death but we can also laugh.

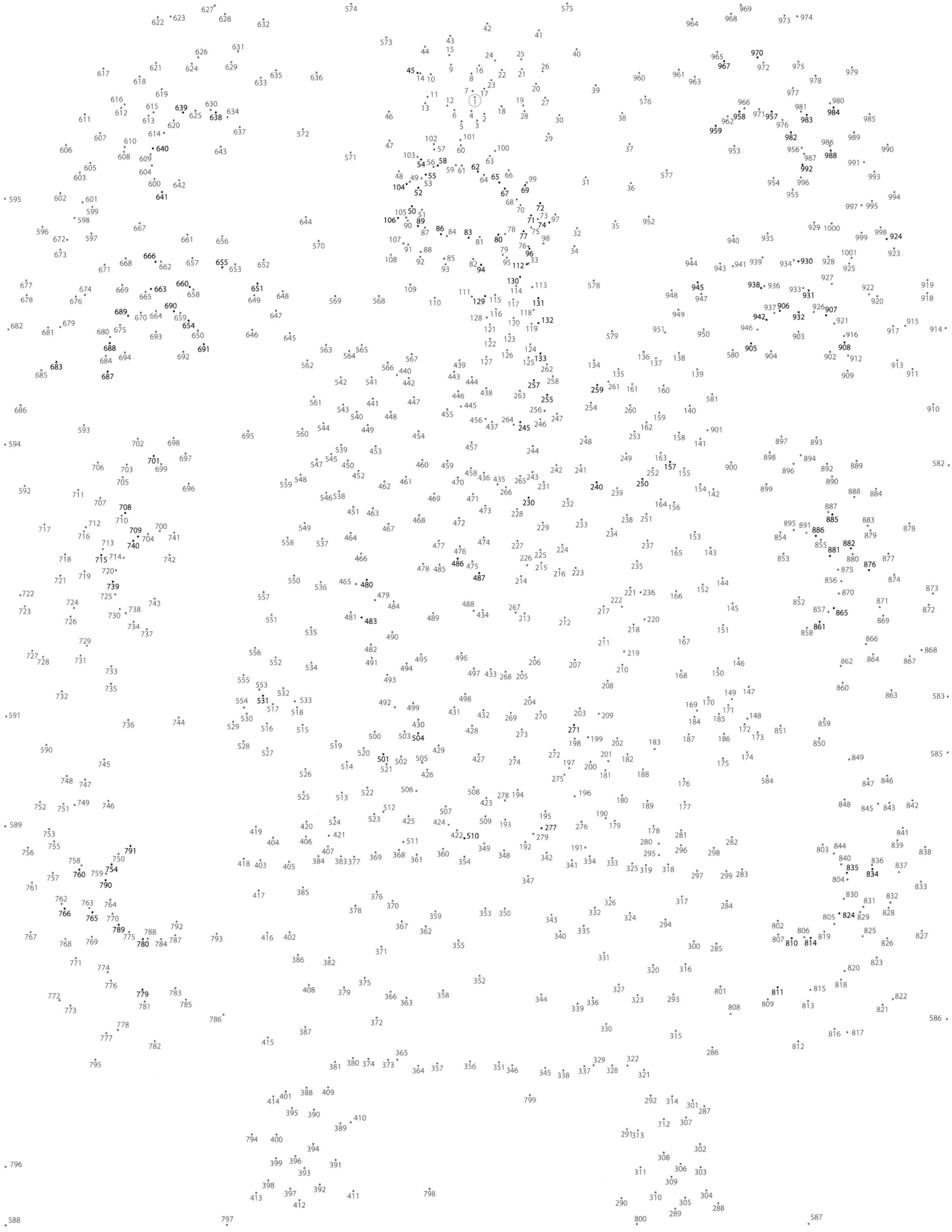

36

Expect to see multiple Catrinas at parades and street parties, accompanied by multiple bridegrooms. For the parade in Mexico City, an event involving the whole community, people will have worked for months creating the elaborate costumes.

37

In some regions, November 1 is the day for costumes. Participants dress in character—priests, devils, widows—and form a funeral procession that goes from house to house, dancing and praying. A brass band accompanies them.

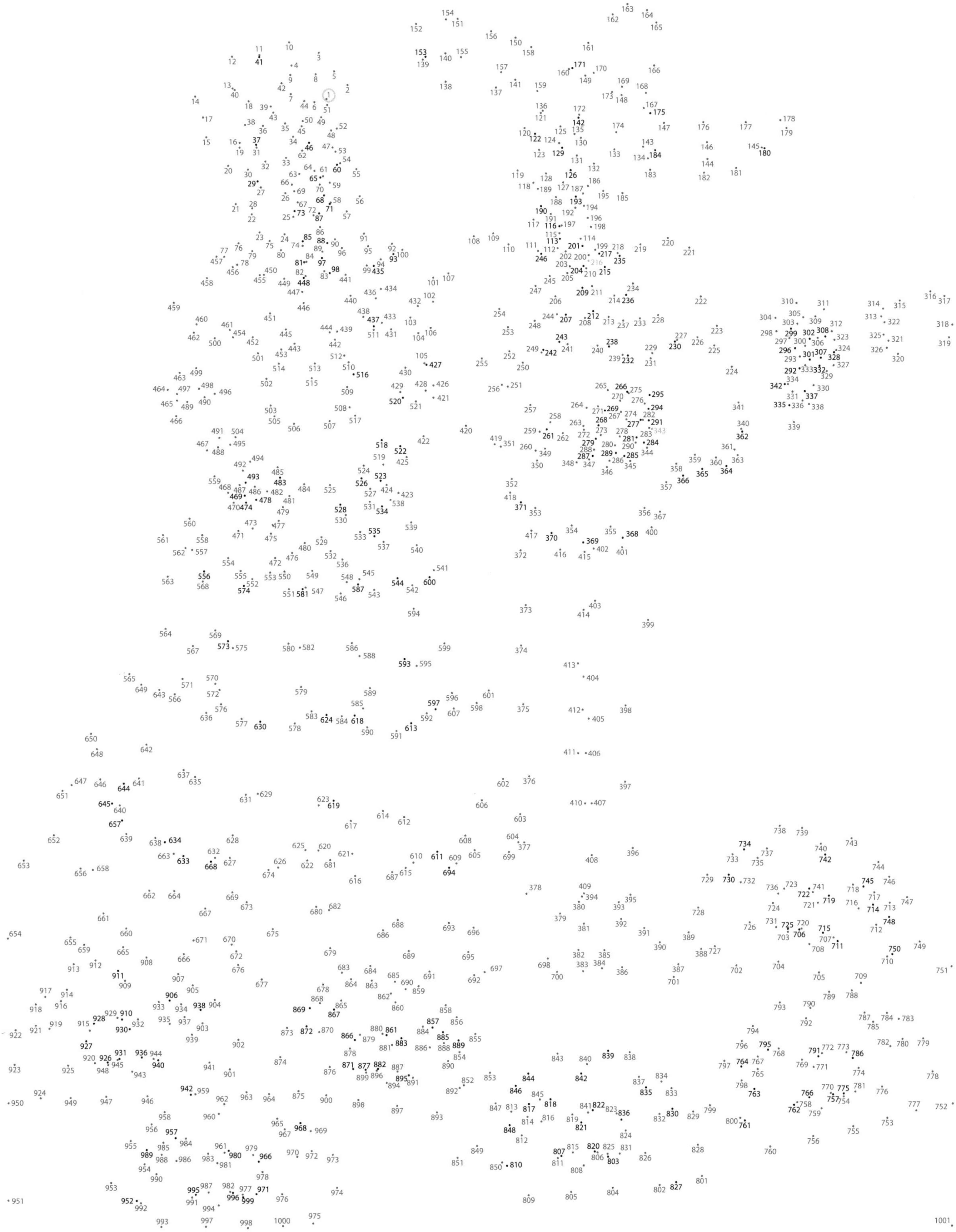

38

The spectacle in Mexico City attracts millions from around the world. No wonder it caught the eye of the producers of the James Bond films. To film their own parade at the start of *Spectre*, they made ten giant skeletons and a quarter of a million paper flowers.

39

The Day of the Dead has only recently become a national holiday in Mexico. The purpose was political: to bring people together via their traditions—even if these were relatively new in some parts of the country where other influences were stronger.

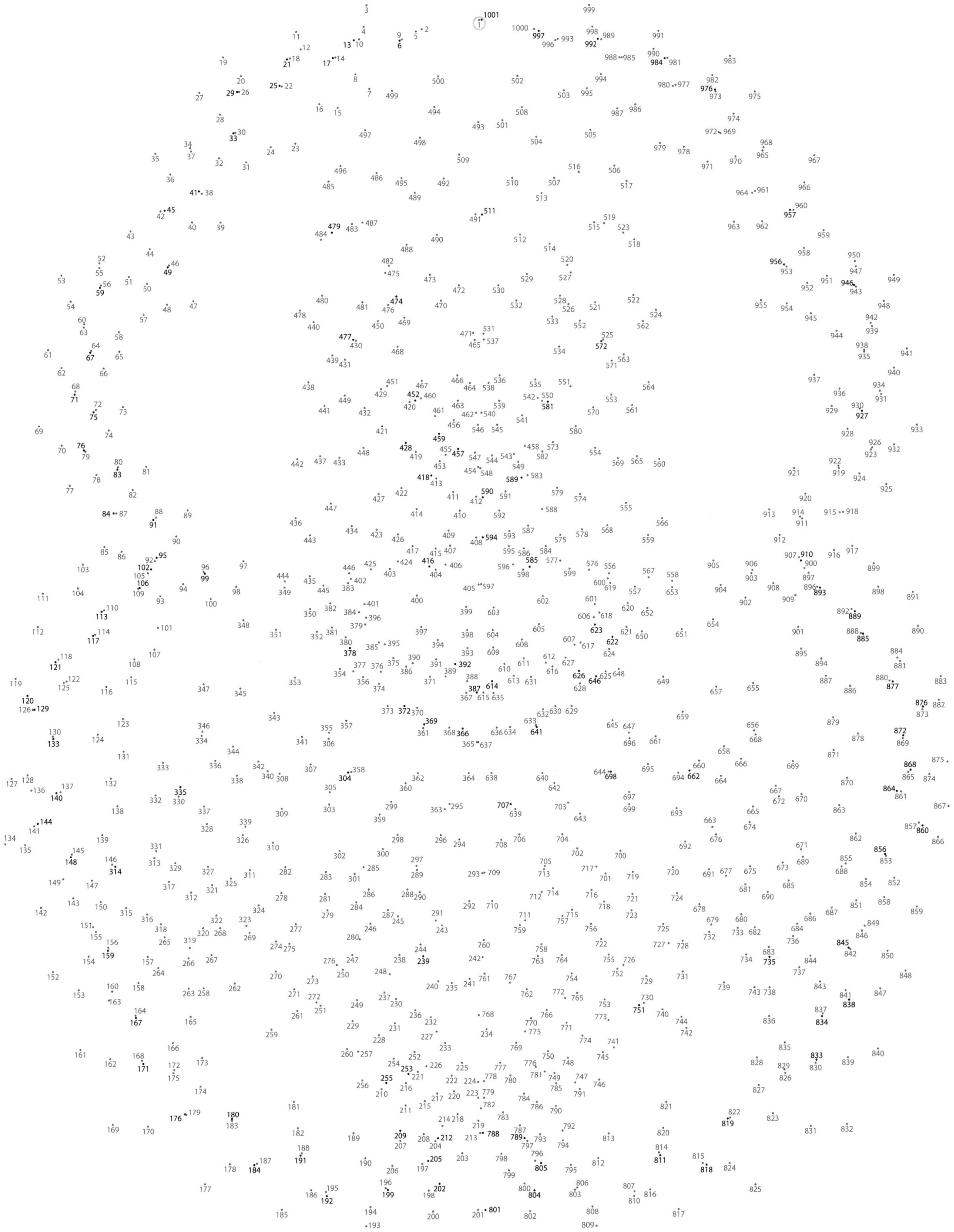

40

The north of Mexico was a region where the Aztec influence was weak, and the Catholic Church's was strong. Rejecting what they regarded as pagan rituals, the people there preferred to celebrate All Souls' Day.

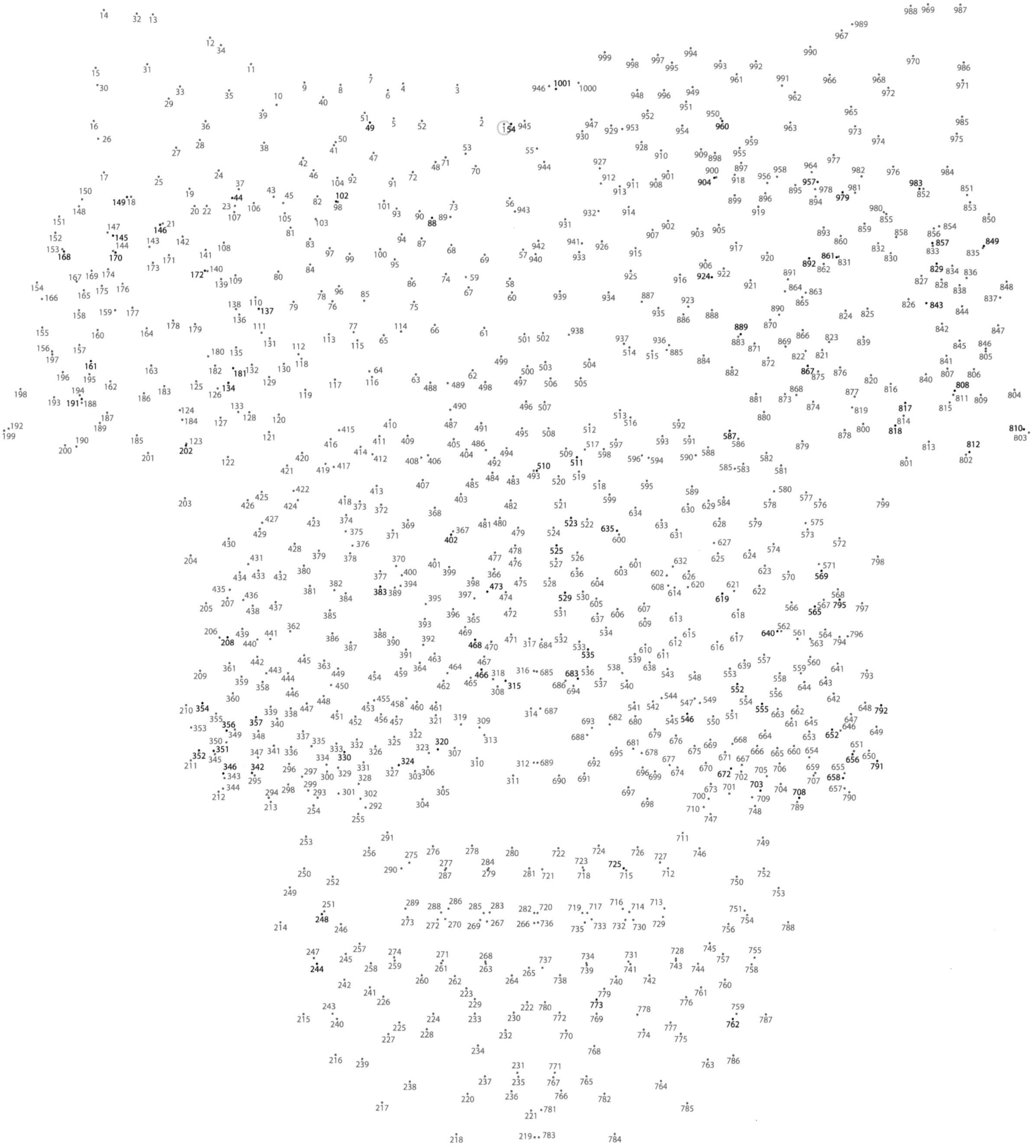

41

Today, the Day of the Dead is also celebrated in the United States. It has traveled wherever Mexicans have settled: Texas, Arizona, and California in particular. The day is often an inclusive celebration of Mexican culture.

42

UNESCO, which aims to protect the world's cultural heritage, put the Day of the Dead on its list of Intangible Cultural Heritage in 2008. By recognizing the value of customs, it hopes to highlight the importance of cultural diversity.

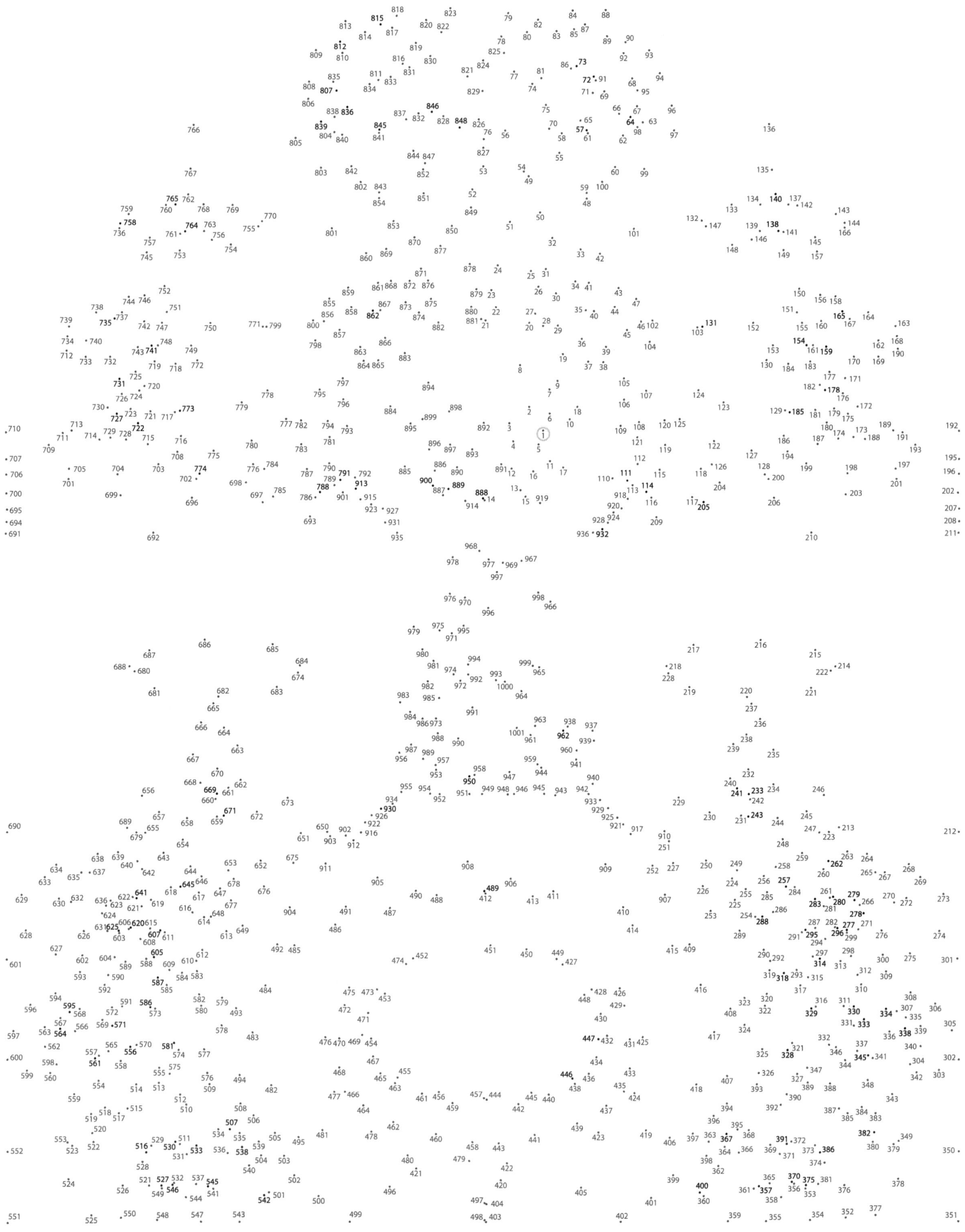

1

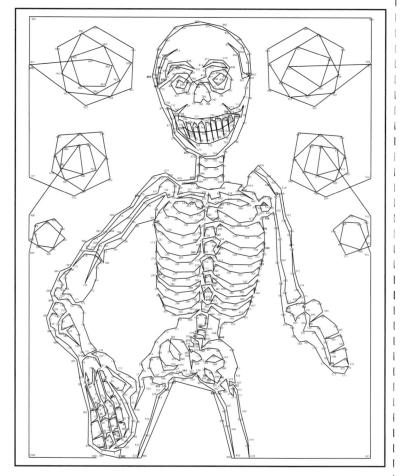

2

3

4

5

6

7

8

9

10

11

12

13

14

15

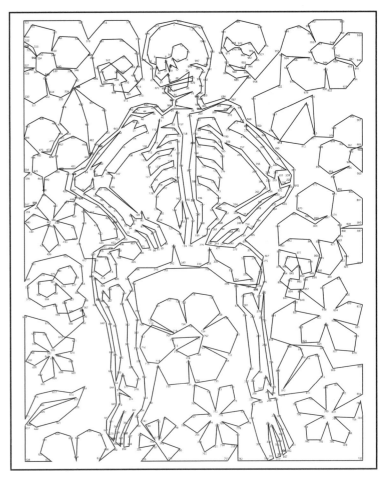

16

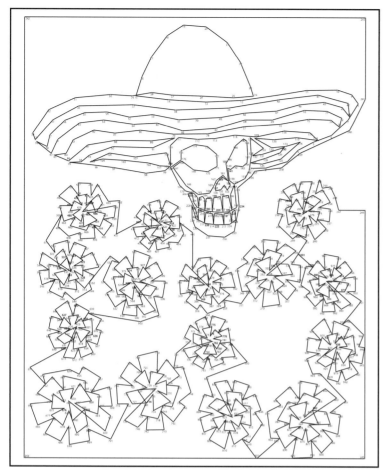

17

18

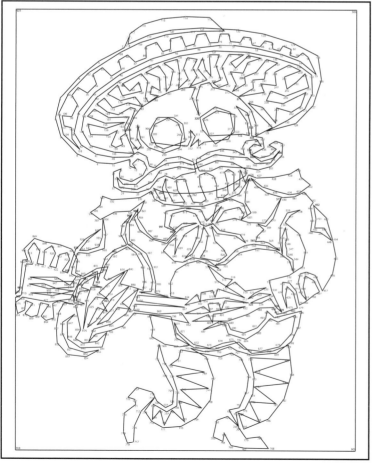

19

20

21

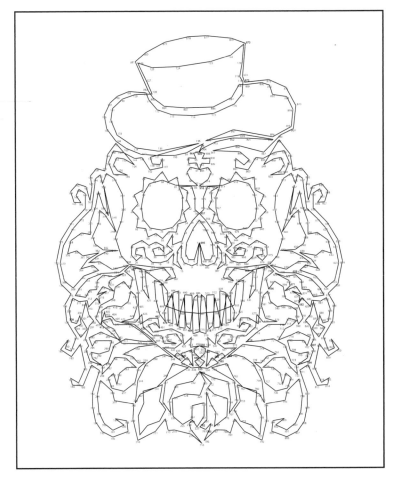

22

23

24

25

26

27

28

29

30

31

32

33

34

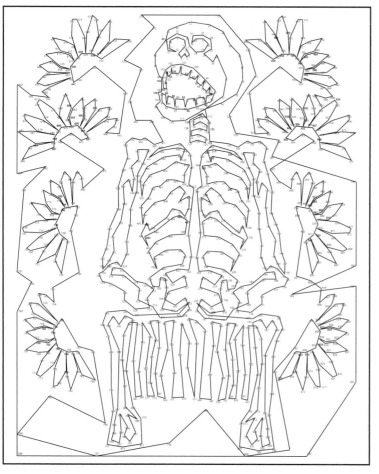

35

36

37

38

39

40

41

42

Thunder Bay Press
Publisher: Peter Norton
Publishing Team: Lori Asbury, Ana Parker, Laura Vignale, Kathryn Chipinka
Editorial Team: JoAnn Padgett, Melinda Allman, Dan Mansfield
Production Team: Jonathan Lopes, Rusty von Dyl

ISBN: 978-1-62686-854-0

Printed in China

20 19 18 17 16   1 2 3 4 5

The publishers would like to thank the following sources for their kind permission to reproduce the pictures in this book.
3. Rvvlada/Shutterstock.com, 5. Gallo Images/Getty Images, 7. Alina Solovyova-Vincent/Getty Images, 9. Jiewsurreal/Shutterstock.com, 11. Alina Solovyova-Vincent/Getty Images, 13. JulianaLoomer/Istockphoto.com, 15. Ivanastar/Istockphoto.com, 17. Jiewsurreal/Shutterstock.com, 19. Agcuesta/Istockphoto.com, 21. & 23. Mofles/Istockphoto.com, 25. Jena_Velour/Shutterstock.com, 27. AGCuesta/Shutterstock.com, 29. NGvozdeva/Istockphoto.com, 31. Jiewsurreal/Shutterstock.com, 33. Danita Delimont/Getty Images, 35. Cvalle/Shutterstock.com, 37. Agcuesta/Shutterstock.com, 39. Christopher Brewer/Shutterstock.com, 41. Vectorfreak/Shutterstock.com, 43. Rvvlada/Shutterstock.com, 45. & 47. Jiewsurreal/Shutterstock.com, 49. Bazzier/Shutterstock.com, 51. Rvvlada/Shutterstock.com, 53. Ira Cvetnaya/Shutterstock.com, 55. Rvvlada/Shutterstock.com, 57. Depiano/Shutterstock.com, 59. Olena Zaskochenko/Shutterstock.com, 61. & 63. Jiewsurreal/Shutterstock.com, 65. Smmartynenko/Shutterstock.com, 67. Alex Rockheart/Shutterstock.com, 69. Olena Zaskochenko/Shutterstock.com, 71. Danefromspain/Istockphoto.com, 73. Jiewsurreal/Shutterstock.com, 75. los_ojos_pardos/Shutterstock.com, 77. NGvozdeva/Shutterstock.com, 79. Daria_I/Shutterstock.com, 81. ARTvektor/Shutterstock.com, 83. Xenia_ok/Shutterstock.com, 85. AGCuesta/Shutterstock.com, 86. (top left) Rvvlada/Shutterstock.com, 86. (top right) Gallo Images/Getty Images, 86. (bottom right) Alina Solovyova-Vincent/Getty Images, 86. (bottom right) Jiewsurreal/Shutterstock.com, 87. (top left) Alina Solovyova-Vincent/Getty Images, 87. (top right) JulianaLoomer/Istockphoto.com, 87. (bottom left) Ivanastar/Istockphoto.com, 87. (bottom right) Jiewsurreal/Shutterstock.com, 88. (top left) Agcuesta/Istockphoto.com, 88. (top right & bottom left) Mofles/Istockphoto.com, 88. (bottom right) Jena_Velour/Shutterstock.com, 89. (top left) AGCuesta/Shutterstock.com, 89. (top right) NGvozdeva/Istockphoto.com, 89. (bottom left) Jiewsurreal/Shutterstock.com, 89. (bottom right) Danita Delimont/Getty Images, 90. (top left) Cvalle/Shutterstock.com, 90. (top right) Agcuesta/Shutterstock.com, 90. (bottom left) Christopher Brewer/Shutterstock.com, 90. (bottom right) Vectorfreak/Shutterstock.com, 91. (top left) Rvvlada/Shutterstock.com, 91. (top right and bottom left) Jiewsurreal/Shutterstock.com, 91. (bottom right) Bazzier/Shutterstock.com, 92. (top left) Rvvlada/Shutterstock.com, 92. (top right) Ira Cvetnaya/Shutterstock.com, 92. (bottom left) Rvvlada/Shutterstock.com, 92. (bottom right) Depiano/Shutterstock.com, 93. (top left) Olena Zaskochenko/Shutterstock.com, 93. (top right & bottom left) Jiewsurreal/Shutterstock.com, 93. (bottom right) Smmartynenko/Shutterstock.com, 94. (top left) Alex Rockheart/Shutterstock.com, 94. (top right) Olena Zaskochenko/Shutterstock.com, 94. (bottom left) Danefromspain/Istockphoto.com, 94. (bottom right) Jiewsurreal/Shutterstock.com, 95. (top left) los_ojos_pardos/Shutterstock.com, 95. (top right) NGvozdeva/Shutterstock.com, 95. (bottom left) Daria_I/Shutterstock.com, 95. (bottom right) ARTvektor/Shutterstock.com, 96. (top left) Xenia_ok/Shutterstock.com, 96. (top right) AGCuesta/Shutterstock.com

Every effort has been made to acknowledge correctly and contact the source and/or copyright holder of each picture, and Carlton Books Limited apologizes for any unintentional errors or omissions, which will be corrected in future editions.